Authenticity

YANETH MEDINA

BOOK SERIES BY FIG FACTOR MEDIA

WordPower Book Series

© Copyright 2021, Fig Factor Media, LLC.
All rights reserved.

All rights reserved. No portion of this book may be reproduced by mechanical, photographic or electronic process, nor may it be stored in a retrieval system, transmitted in any form or otherwise be copied for public use or private use without written permission of the copyright owner.

It is sold with the understanding that the publisher and the individual authors are not engaged in the rendering of psychological, legal, accounting or other professional advice. The content and views in each chapter are the sole expression and opinion of its author and not necessarily the views of Fig Factor Media, LLC.

For more information, contact:

Fig Factor Media, LLC | www.figfactormedia.com

Cover Design & Layout by Juan Pablo Ruiz
Printed in the United States of America

ISBN: 978-1-957058-12-2
Library of Congress Control Number: 2021923764

DEDICATION

I dedicate this book to my beloved parents who raised me to be the person I am today. They continue to demonstrate what being authentic means. I would like to continue the legacy of my parents to my boys and all of the people whose lives I touch.

ACKNOWLEDGMENTS

I have to start by thanking my wonderful parents who have always been there for me and everyone in our family. They are the most kind, humble, and caring humans I know. Despite not having large corporate salaries, they found ways to help others while raising us. They were and will continue to be my inspiration! I also want to send a special thanks to my mentor at the bank who helped me see my talent and leadership. He helped me realize that my authentic self would lead to success. I would be remiss to not mention Sandi, my professional and personal coach. She has always told me I could go far. I always had that power and it took several years to see it. Sandi, you are a wonderful coach, and you changed my world—thank you! Lastly, I am eternally grateful to Jackie Camacho-Ruiz. She has given me so many beautiful experiences. To be an author for the third time is just surreal! Her heart beeps and so does mine! Thank you for elevating me and all of the amazing people you touch. You are our angel!

INTRO

It is truly an amazing feeling to be publishing another book with fabulous authors who transcend and provide great insight on their word power! When the beautiful Jacqueline Camacho-Ruiz asked me, I was not sure what word I wanted to select; so many came to my mind. Then I visualized my new t-shirt bought in honor of Hispanic Heritage Month. I was drawn to this shirt for the powerful words listed on it. One out of the four words stood out to me: "Auténtica" or, "Authentic."

I chose "authenticity" because I have always stayed true to myself and have tried my best to influence kids, my family, and my team at work. People who know me know that I am genuine and will always do what I can to help others. Words cannot express how grateful I am to be doing this book. My goal is to have you realize that being authentic can be so rewarding just like it has been for me.

THE MEANING

Authenticity is defined as: "Not false or copied; genuine; real." And…. "Representing one's true nature or beliefs; true to oneself or to the person identified."

To be your authentic self is when your words, actions, and behaviors consistently match your identity! People can feel, hear, and see your actions. They have an emotional connection with you and you are seen as a trustworthy person. Your individuality is seen in all of these acts. This is what separates you from others. People can almost anticipate how you will act when they have that emotional connection.

Here are ways you can demonstrate that you are authentic:
- Sharing your opinion honestly
- Aligning your decisions with your beliefs
- Acting from your heart (Yes, people will see it once they know you!)
- Being unafraid and vulnerable
- No matter if it's good or bad news, always being transparent

SELF-REFLECTION

First, I think it is important to do some self-reflection and dive deeply into your inner soul: Are you authentic? Do you know? Do you come across as an authentic person? Do people see you as a genuine person who truly cares about others including yourself?

Knowing who we are is fundamental to understanding ourselves. It is even more important that we are aware of what we send out to the world as this impacts our lives. Awareness builds the relationships in our personal life and in the workplace. We are all authentic as children, taught to be nice, respectful, and caring. Yet as we grow, circumstances and society divert us from being authentic or lead us to believe that there are things far more important than being your authentic self. Don't be fooled. Let's embark on finding *you!*

BE YOU!

Simply put... Be you! Authenticity is about representing your true self or beliefs. Don't be shy or afraid to show the world who you are. Be proud of who you are. Talk about what's important to you and be prepared to say why. If there is something that you believe is unique to you, talk about it. Some people say actions speak louder than words, but that is not always the case. In my opinion, words are equally important. Sharing your thoughts, ideas, and personal opinions are also a way to be authentic. Cumulatively, you are creating your own brand. People follow those they connect with. Be YOU! It is that simple. Be your authentic self!

THE PASSION

"When you're authentic, you end up following your heart, and you put yourself in places and situations and in conversations that you love and that you enjoy. You meet people that you like talking to. You go places you've dreamt about. And you end up following your heart and feeling very fulfilled."
– NEIL PASRICHA, Author of You Are Awesome

Authentic people are passionate. They discover that their internal motivator is their heart. They know when to follow their heart. Their intuition is driven by their heart. They thrive off success stories that come from the heart. The biggest reward for them is to see how they helped make an impact. This passion is when trust and self-confidence grow. Genuine relationships are built with likeminded, passionate people who support you for who you really are. Start to cultivate this now!

THE DO'S AND THE DON'TS

When you are aware of what authenticity looks like, you can quickly point out the qualities of a person who is authentic versus someone who is clearly not. Here are some qualities of the two personalities.

An authentic person will:
- Be Transparent
- Express Gratitude
- Show that he or she cares by their actions
- Will demonstrate by actions that this is about the team and themselves
- Lives their word
- Listens and allows collaboration

A person who is not authentic will:
- Be perceived as dishonest or unwilling to be open
- Is inconsistent with communication to the team
- Always talk themselves up instead of celebrating
- Gossips

FACE YOUR FEARS

When you are developing your authentic self, your fears may come into play. Therefore, it is important that you have the courage to face your fears. One thing you can do to combat fear is look at yourself and identify your core beliefs. What do you want to convey to the world? What is most important to you? Once identified, talk about those beliefs. Be transparent, even if it feels strange. Your heart may race or your hands may sweat but you are starting to speak freely about what you believe in. So as much as possible, and as slowly as you need to, courageously talk about it and invigorate your *Authentic Self*.

LOVE

"Love encompasses a range of strong and positive emotional and mental states, from the most sublime virtue or good habit, the deepest interpersonal affection, to the simplest pleasure."

Wikipedia does a great job describing how love is correlated with virtues or good habits. The authentic person's acts come from within their inner soul. They act from the goodness of their heart. It is about the love in giving to others while practicing self-love. It is one of their greatest virtues. These good habits eventually become second nature. Once we master love, we understand we are connected and will always give a helping hand. Genuine love of helping others drives us to love even more!

Try it and see the benefits!

Source: https://en.wikipedia.org/wiki/Love

LEADERSHIP

If you want to take your leadership to higher levels, be authentic and keep it simple. Your team wants to know you genuinely care about them. They crave to be noticed. Take the time to appreciate them in all facets of their career. Celebrate milestones, no matter how big or small. Tell them that you appreciate them. Let them know in-person when you see something you like. Email your boss highlighting any team or individual success stories so they know you care and acknowledge their work. Be your coworkers' advocate and talk them up in the board room! An authentic leader has a heart that cares. Their actions show this. People will work hard for leaders who demonstrate that they care about them. Remember this…

"Authenticity is your most precious commodity as a leader."
– MARCUS BUCKINGHAM.

Take care of this treasure and lead to greatness!

LA PRESIDENTA!

A young Latina migrated to the United States at two years old. In kindergarten, this little girl did not know a word of English, yet with persistence and authenticity, she rose up in the banking world. Despite many barriers, I am proud to say that I am that little girl, now La Presidenta of the bank!

I directly link my success to authenticity. The team sees me as a person who truly cares, communicates, listens, and welcomes feedback. During tough times, I showed vulnerability. Together we were stronger—that was our message. We always celebrated success. Our culture was about "us," never about "me." It was a culture of winning. To have achieved this level in my career brings me great joy! My heart is full of gratitude, and I feel blessed with the impact of my leadership! How will you take your authenticity and build your winning team?

THE REWARDS!

"I had no idea that being your authentic self could make me as rich as I've become. If I had, I'd have done it a lot earlier."
- OPRAH WINFREY.

Let me be clear. History has shown that being authentic will bring you rewards. But a true authentic person does not do things for their own benefit. They do it for others. When people recognize your authentic acts and great intentions, an emotional connection happens. Thus, here is a great example of how Oprah's connected with the entire country through authenticity. She did things because she genuinely cared. She was true to herself and gave without expecting in return. The moral of this story is that being authentic is an intangible asset that can bring rewards to our life. Always remember that!

THE AUTHENTIC YOU

Here is a great 3-step process to help you reflect and discover your authentic self!

KNOW YOUR STRENGTHS!

- What comes naturally to you that you are really good at?
- Ask your friends and family: what strengths do they see in you?
- Review your strengths and embrace them

DO WHAT YOU LOVE!

- It's that simple: do what you love!
- Make a conscious effort to do this and make no excuse.
- When you love what you do, your work will show it!

BE HAPPY WITH YOURSELF!

- Love everything about yourself!
- If there is something that you don't like, work on it!
- The key: always be happy with you!

Be Fearlessly Authentic!

ABOUT THE AUTHOR

Yaneth Medina serves as the President of Elgin for St Charles Bank & Trust Company, N.A, a Wintrust Community Bank. Yaneth has more than 25 years of experience in leadership, banking, relationship building, workplace culture, and coaching and mentoring. She wears many hats and serves on many internal committees, including business development, compliance, and employee recognition. She also sits on several corporate level committees.

Yaneth's strong work ethic and integrity have helped her achieve in her career. She is also viewed by colleagues as a supportive member of the management team and she understands the value of promoting and inspiring a positive culture in which everyone can thrive.

She also dedicates her time to serving several organizations in the local area. Currently, she is the Vice President/Board Member for Centro De Informacion, a non-for-profit agency whose mission is to empower Hispanics with the ability to effectively integrate into our greater community through the facilitation of information, education, citizenship and well-being. Additionally, Yaneth serves as Chair/Board Member for the Elgin Area Chamber of Commerce. Finally, Yaneth is also on the board & Finance Committee of Marklund, a non-for-profit organization that serves infants, children, teens and adults with serious and profound developmental disabilities and special healthcare needs.

Yaneth's Award Recognitions:
- Latina Style Magazine| Top 10 Corporate LATINA Executives of the year for 2019
- Today's Inspired Latina| Today's Inspired Latina Woman of the Year for 2020
- Illinois State Treasurer| Outstanding Commitment in Community Service for 2021

Yaneth's family consists of her three wonderful boys, her parents, and her brother and sister. They have been her inspiration!

www.ingramcontent.com/pod-product-compliance
Lightning Source LLC
Chambersburg PA
CBHW040021300426
43673CB00107B/338